FOR PEOPLES WEARY OF IN

HEALING PRAYERS · & MEDITATIONS

To resist a violent world

By Dennae Pierre

HEALING PRAYERS & MEDITATIONS

To resist a violent world

This collection of meditations is for all striving under weights of oppression
For peoples weary of injustice and those healing from violence
Prayers to guide our resistance

By Dennae Pierre

Healing Prayers & Meditations to resist a violent world (1st Ed.)

Published by Dennae Pierre
4743 E Mariposa St.
Phoenix, Arizona 85018

© 2020 by Dennae Pierre
Cover design by Michael & Nia Ajayi
Artwork by Anthony Vasquez
"Birds" artwork by Nicole Davy

Published 2020.
Printed in the United States of America

ISBN: 978-0-578-74159-8

CON-
TENTS

INVITATION

REPENTANCE AND LAMENTS

HEALING JOURNEYS

Introduction

Over the years, I have belonged to various socio-economically and ethnically diverse communities desiring to live in reconciliation with one another, while seeking God's justice and peace in our cities. It has been beautiful and painful, relationally rich and relationally devastating, momentous and ordinary, costly and priceless. Together we have entered into spaces of individual and communal suffering, hoping to see God's light break into unjust and unrighteous "powers and principalities" that lurk in the shadows of individuals, families, systems, and institutions. We want communities to flourish and experience wholeness. We share a conviction that God's people are called to be a faithful witness to Jesus, as we announce the kingdom of God—most especially in places where the shadows of hell are visible on earth.

It is not enough to describe the brokenness of the world. It is not enough to speak against injustice. It is not enough to resist evil. Yes, God's people are called to do all these things; but if we are to truly see peace, justice, and reconciliation embodied by God's people, we must awaken to the reality of our union with Jesus, and our intimate and holy connection to one another. If we can begin to envision and even experience what is waiting on the other side of seeking justice and righteousness, we will not only resist evil, but our motivation to do so will come from experiencing union and deep communion with God, others, and self.

Our fractured selves cannot remain present in our own suffering—let alone the suffering of others—without an immense amount of exhaustion. Eventually, we burn out. Eventually, we hurt those around us through self-righteousness, pride, and anger. Or eventually, we give up and comply with the way things are—unless we take an alternate path. This path invites us to remain present in suffering and resist injustice, as it deepens our yearning for restored relationship with all mankind.

This ache touches on the deepest parts of who we are—our desires, longings, and most significant needs. It uncovers the parts of us that need God's healing touch and exposes the parts of our story that are still in need of hearing God's truth. If we are to engage in God's work with a posture that looks like Jesus, then we need God's healing and renewal. Some of this healing is mysterious, personal, and done in secret between us and God, but not most of it. God more often chooses to heal us by dispensing his infinite love through mankind and allowing us to lavish one another with his divine love. We experience healing as we are seen and see one another through the eyes of Christ.

All those themes are represented in three sections of this prayer book: Invitation, Repentance and Laments, and Healing Journeys.

Part One: Invitation - These prayers are an invitation to let the reality of God's kingdom saturate our senses. If we allow our vision of "the way things are supposed to be" become indescribable and yet viscerally known within us, then our longing for Christ's kingdom becomes almost unbearable. It is with this vision intact that we can lament the effect injustice, oppression, and individual sin has on what Rev. Martin Luther King Jr described as *the beloved community*, a society based on God's justice, equality, and deep love for all humanity.

Part Two: Repentance and Laments - This collection of prayers and meditations is designed to give language to communities that are weary of injustice. They are prayers to remain in suffering while learning to abide in Christ. They are confessions that expose the harm we do to one another while trusting God's forgiveness and mercy to heal us.

Part Three: Healing Journeys - Repentance and lament are intended to be the kind of prayers that allow for deeper encounters with God. Wherever that does not happen it is because we are living within distorted stories. God's healing presence in our lives re-narrates his truth over the most painful parts of our lives. This is the inner work necessary to engage long term in the ministry of justice and reconciliation in ways that reflect Jesus.

This is a book of prayers written for my community in the midst of a significant season of sorrow and loss. A global pandemic, growing economic insecurity, and the obvious disparity in health and death rates among the wealthy and poor have filled our headlines. But for those ministering in particular contexts, it has meant non-stop caring for those experiencing sickness, dying, death, and loss. In addition, multiple murders of black men and women by police officers, culminating with George Floyd, caused another spark in the racial justice movement that this time erupted into wildfire. All the while, we continue to watch many parts of the church take a defensive posture to shifting cultural norms while doubting, biting, and devouring one another.

As God prunes his church, something new seems to be birthing among God's people in the United States. This book is an attempt to invite us to envision, repent, heal, and experience deeper communion as we dispense God's love, justice, and mercy in the midst of a violent world.

My prayer for those who spend time with this book is that the words and art would create space to encounter beauty, conviction, healing, and longing for God's kingdom to be visible on earth as it is in heaven.

– Dennae Pierre

INVITATION

pt.1

BELOVED COMMUNION

ENTER

THE

GATES

Of this beloved communion
Where you find
The marvelous saints

Displaced and hungry
short life and cold nights
in prison and dark allies
I found them

Blessed are they
The Poor in Spirit

Enter the gates
of this beloved communion
where you meet saints
weeping in union

Lost life, broken bodies
awake to the world's pain
ruptures in fellowship
bring them such pain

BLESSED ARE

THEY WHO

MOURN

Enter the gates
of this beloved communion
where you find
the art of surrender

Humble they released
pursuit of man's praise
grips on riches and pleasure
instead they found me, their treasure

Blessed are they
The Meek

Enter the gates
of this beloved communion
filled with contagious zeal
where you'll meet my delight

Parched and famished
longing for restored humanity
satisfied and quenched
through feasting on me, their bread

Blessed are they
Who Crave Righteousness

Enter the gates
of this beloved communion
where weak and wounded,
enjoying and strengthening one other

Wounds and limps exposed
radiating mercy
they generously give
all that they are, in worship

      Blessed are they
          The Merciful

Enter the gates
of this beloved communion
discover the ones who see
the invisible

They look into the eyes
of the unwanted and lonely
seeing Me, they call them "Holy"
welcoming the abandoned as family

      Blessed are they
          The Pure in Heart

Enter the gates
of this beloved communion
meet my children
radiating the beauty of joy

Through hostility and assault
they found each other
subverting abusive power through love
they remain like little ones

BLESSED ARE

THEY —————————

MY PEACEMAKERS

Enter the gates
of this beloved communion
find the martyrs, the abandoned, rejected
loyal to me, they won't conform to false kingdoms

Resisting the darkness
they open windows so others can see
into my kingdom of light
their only desired reward, this beloved communion

Blessed are they
The Persecuted

Enter the gates
of this beloved communion
find my children
pouring my love
into one another

Blessed are you
My Saints

KINGDOM VISION

Give me a vision

of your kingdom

I want eyes to see

your people, glorious

unhindered by lies

freedom to love

Abundance flows

Ordinary people
lonely people
awkward people
even grumpy people

Are redeemed
laughing, rejoicing in love
Give me a vision of your kingdom
I want eyes to see
where what once was treasured
now lays at your feet
delighting in the treasure
given to us in the Holy Brethren

Give me a vision of your kingdom
Tears wiped away
by tender hands
and listening ears
of other saints
Christ's compassion flowing

Give me a vision of your kingdom
As we remember
abused and worn bodies
weak, old, and young
sick and strong
limping done
all radiating Christ's love

Give me a vision of your kingdom
Where no amount of
wealth, praise, or power
can possibly replace
the holy wonder
of unity with God
Give me a vision of your kingdom
when secret things
are exposed in love's perfect light
no longer ashamed
we marvel and stand
that we've been made clean

Give me a vision of your kingdom
delighting in you
and you in us
with each other
one with you
sharing all things in common
receiving from you our daily bread

Lord give me a vision of your kingdom
words to describe
to those far off and alone
Disgusted by religion
Tired of the rules
Worn out from addictions
burdened and weary
from the siren's song
They are welcome
to arrive at your shores
and delight in pure love
Greeted by our Lord

CAN THE WEALTHY FOLLOW JESUS?

the call is not merely to encounter him

Can the wealthy of this world find Jesus?
Can the powerful come to him?
Yes
But the call is not merely to encounter him,
But to follow
Which requires a different cost

They arrive with layers of protection
They hide their nakedness behind
Expensive clothing
Robes of self-made righteousness
Purchased with power and wealth
It comforts them
Gives them security
Belonging
A false sense of endless life
But eventually the powerful
Realize even with layers

Bodies grow weak
Loved ones get sick
Children die
And money cannot fix
Broken marriages or addictions

Are the weak and despised of the world more righteous?
Are they more holy because they're poor?
No
But they arrive naked, hungry and excluded
They are seen
Jesus is their reward

They arrive in scraps
Barely hiding their nakedness
Behind tattered clothes from unrighteous blows
Resisting injustice or simply trying to exist
They too crave comfort
Protection, power
Belonging and to be seen
To escape from their tired life
But all they have are scraps to grasp

are they more

holy

because

they're poor?

Jesus tells their weak bodies, "Welcome"
He bids the outcast, join
He raises children from the dead
And provides them their daily bread
He shines light into senseless actions

Jesus tells the wealthy, leave it and follow me.

Jesus tells the wealthy, leave it and follow me.

Jesus tells the wealthy, leave it and follow me.

Jesus tells the wealthy, leave it and follow me.

Jesus tells the wealthy, leave it and follow me.

Jesus tells the wealthy, leave it and follow me.

Jesus tells the wealthy, leave it and follow me
Because he loves them
And knows their robes of righteousness
And false security
Can never save them or satisfy their deepest longings
Their hoarding harms his weak sons and daughters

Jesus tells the despised of the world, "Come in!"
Beloved, raise your head high
Let go of the scraps,
Though terrifying
Put on my robes
Come, be my sons and daughters!"

Powerful and poor stand level
Before the throne of God
They encounter the same Christ
Who knows them
Makes to each a differnt ask

The rich young ruler
Walked away sad
His wealth too great
But his beloved daughter
Pushed her way in
Passing by the judgment
Weeping at his feet

Perhaps on another day
The woman, Christ's disciple
And the rich young ruler,
Encountered each other
What might she say?
To give him hope
That even though he lost
It wasn't too late
To follow the light of life
And join her
As a beloved brother

BEAUTY

I need beauty

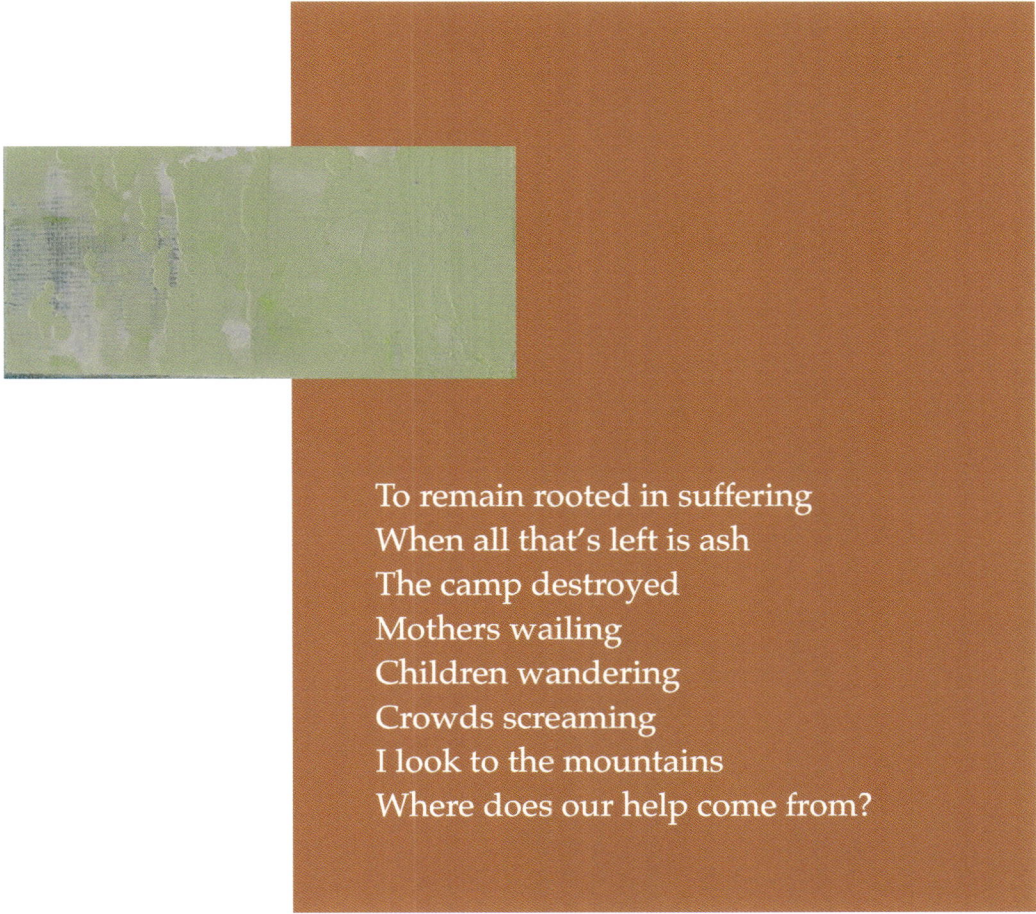

To remain rooted in suffering
When all that's left is ash
The camp destroyed
Mothers wailing
Children wandering
Crowds screaming
I look to the mountains
Where does our help come from?

I need beauty
As smoke rises
From the valley below
And my heart aches
Knowing I must go
Into the valley
To sit with loved ones
Who have lost all
To weep, lament, and be
I look for beauty
Lead me by the quiet streams

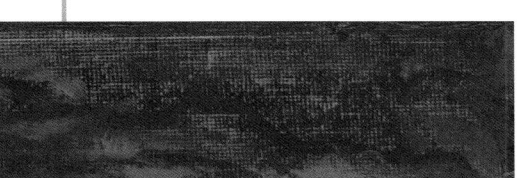

Glorious mountains stand tall
Looking over generations of oppression
And spilt blood
Flowers emerge from cracks
And rocks and mud
Where battles rage
The curious smile of a tender child
Brightens gray days
To enter in the suffering
I must open up
To beauty

"the violence un-
folding is not the
end of our story"

The sounds of rushing water
Glimpses of green forests
Blue skies
Anything that sings,
 "The violence unfolding
is not the end of our story"

I will sit here and be honest about the pain
Never can I leave behind
The suffering of our people
Grow me in endurance
Press me further in
Carrying burdens
Christ carries with me
By giving me
His beauty

SACRED UNION

At first I met you
In the mystery
Of holy transformation
When I exchanged my robe
For your dirty rags
Glorious was that day

Remember how we walked
Just you and I
Through dark valleys
And raging seas
To bring you here
Because it's not enough to save you
From damnation, eternal separation
But to know me
Is to know my joy
The fellowship inside me

Union is no abstraction
Divorced from embodied action
But as you enter deeper
Into my communion
Greater healing will be found
In the treasures I've hidden
Within the brethren all around

To know me more intimately
I now need you to trust
That I am not satisfied with
Merely private encounter
But because I want you fully seen
I brought you to this place
To encounter others face to face

no need to hide

No need to hide
Like you, they were once lost
But now they're found and inhabit me
And there are depths of you
I want to reach
And I will do it
Through the flesh of my beloved saints

There is something much greater
Than euphoria you have known in moments
And it is to be deeply seen
And see
Within my sacred union

Among my saints
Be a fellow sinner
There is no need to hide
Or protect

It is within this fellowship
That I will fight
For you to be seen
By each other
It is here that I will contend
For your soul to emerge
Content
Receiving and giving love
Within my sacred union

UNITY IS SOLIDARITY

Unity

It's as real as flesh and blood
God did not step back and wait
To abstractly create
A people for himself
But through the covenant
And the incarnation
The Word became
Flesh and blood
Making us one with him

Every tribe, people, and tongue
Make up this
Holy breathtaking communion
Once a people far off
Enemies to his Holy name
Now called and loved
Knit together by his blood

Unity

A mystical space
We share with Christ
But not him alone
It includes
One another
And is known
Through sacrifice
Finding those pushed to the edge
By injustice
By darkness and destruction
Caring for the weakest parts
Speaking up for those ignored

Unity

Is submitting power to one another
Searching for ways to place yourself
Underneath the other
To look for those discarded
Unwanted, not needed
To go find them, bring them in,
Put them at the center

Sacrifice

To serve the weaker brother
And enjoy the unwanted sister
The lowly and abandoned
The peoples put in prison
The skin that is assaulted
Must be brought to
The center of our communion
As we learn to receive
The glorious reunion
That comes as we live
In union learning to practice

Solidarity

REPENTANCE

Repentance
It's not quite like
Being a child
Standing before your parents
"Fess up, what have you done?"
The scolding father asks
What he already knows
But waits silently
Forcing confession
With his angry gaze
A pit rises in your stomach
Say you're sorry
Get on with the punishment
This is not repentance

Repentance is more like
Being a child
Hiding under your covers
Scared to come out
Fearful of being discovered
Your heart beats fast
You hear Dad's voice
Sinking deeper into hiding
He gently calls again,
You peek out
And right there all along
Has been your loving Father
Present, patiently waiting
To pull you on his lap
Listening to you honestly
Share what happened
So he can tell you
The good news story
Transforming every part of you
Freeing you to deeply love
Your sisters and your brothers

Repentance is a sacred gift
It is invitation to let go, discover
The love of your Father,
"Beloved, you're welcome here
You belong, no need to hide
Let's grieve together
Where things went wrong
Don't fear your guilt."

Uncovering is only the beginning
The joy is to see
Christ's face
Enraptured by his lavish love
Found in fellowship
With his sons and daughters
Come learn the tender dance
Of repentance
Tasting the sweeter union
You will have with God and man

The fire of God's love exists
So that it can uncover all covers
Revealing what is hidden
For the purpose of God's Holy Light
Telling you His truth
That every part of you
Loved and cloaked in Christ's union
Is invited to transformation
So that you might taste
Deeper communion
With his Holy Saints

uncover all covers

REPENTANCE
AND LAMENTS
pt.2

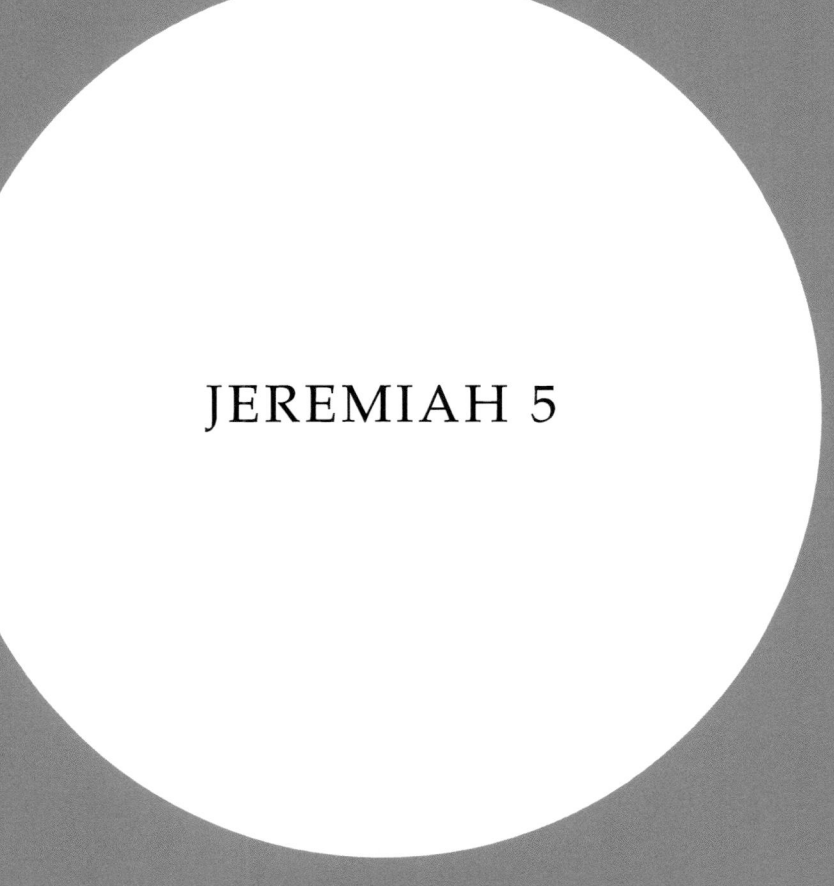

JEREMIAH 5

"Go up and down the streets of Jerusalem,
	look around and consider,
		search through her squares.
If you can find but one person
who deals honestly and seeks the truth,
		I will forgive this city.
2 Although they say, 'As surely as the Lord
l	i	v	e	s	,	'
		still they are swearing falsely."

3 Lord, do not your eyes look for truth?
	You struck them, but they felt no pain;
	you crushed them, but they refused
c	o	r	r	e	c	t	i	o	n	.
They made their faces harder than stone
		and	refused	to	repent.
4 I thought, "These are only the poor;
			they	are	foolish,
for they do not know the way of the Lord,
		the requirements of their God.
5 So I will go to the leaders
			and	speak	to	them;
surely they know the way of the Lord,
		the requirements of their God."
But with one accord they too had broken
off			the			yoke
		and torn off the bonds.
6 Therefore a lion from the forest will
attack					them,
	a wolf from the desert will ravage them,
a leopard will lie in wait near their towns
	to tear to pieces any who venture out,
for
			their backslidings many.

7	"Why should I forgive you?
	Your children have forsaken
	and sworn by gods that are not gods.
I	supplied	all	their	needs,
			yet they committed adultery
	and thronged to the houses of prosti-
t	u	t	e	s	.
8 They are well-fed, lusty stallions,
	each neighing for another man's wife.
9 Should I not punish them for this?"
			declares	the	Lord.
"Should	I	not	avenge	myself
		on such a nation as this?

10 "Go through her vineyards and ravage
t	h	e	m	,

but do not destroy them completely.
Strip	off	her	branches,
	for these people do not belong to the
L			o			r			d			.
11 The people of Israel and the people of
J		u		d		a		h
	have been utterly unfaithful to me,"
declares			the			Lord.

12 They have lied about the Lord;
	they said, He will do nothing!
No	harm	will	come	to	us;
	we will never see sword or famine.
13 The prophets are but wind
	and the word is not in them;
	so let what they say be done to them."
14 Therefore this is what the Lord God
Almighty says:

"Because the people have spoken these
w		o		r		d		s	,
	I will make my words in your mouth a fire
	and these people the wood it consumes.
15 People of Israel," declares the Lord,
	"I am bringing a distant nation against
y			o			u			—
an	ancient	and	enduring	nation,
	a people whose language you do not
k		n		o		w		,
	whose speech you do not understand.
16 Their quivers are like an open grave;
		all of them are mighty warriors.
17 They will devour your harvests and food,
		devour your sons and daughters;
they will devour your flocks and herds,
		devour your vines and fig trees.
With	the	sword	they	will	destroy
	the fortified cities in which you trust.

18 "Yet even in those days," declares the
Lord, "I will not destroy you completely. 19
And when the people ask, 'Why has the
Lord our God done all this to us?' you will
tell them, 'As you have forsaken me and
served foreign gods in your own land, so
now you will serve foreigners in a land not
your					own.'

20 "Announce this to the descendants of
J		a		c		o		b

and proclaim it in Judah:
21 Hear this, you foolish and senseless
p e o p l e ,
   who have eyes but do not see,
   who have ears but do not hear:
22 Should you not fear me?" declares the
L o r d .
   "Should you not tremble in my presence?
I made the sand a boundary for the sea,
   an everlasting barrier it cannot cross.
The waves may roll, but they cannot
p r e v a i l ;
   they may roar, but they cannot cross it.
23 But these people have stubborn and
rebellious   hearts;
   they have turned aside and gone.
24 They do not say to themselves,
   'Let us fear the Lord our God,
who gives autumn and spring rains
s e a s o n ,
   who assures us of the regular weeks of
h a r v e s t .'
25 Your wrongdoings have kept these
a w a y ;
   your sins have deprived you of good.

   "Among my people are the wicked
who lie in wait like men who snare birds
and like those who set traps to catch
p e o p l e .
   Like cages full of birds,
   their houses are full of deceit;
they have become rich and powerful
   and have grown fat and sleek.
Their evil deeds have no limit;
   they do not seek justice.
They do not promote the case of the father-
l e s s ;
   they do not defend the just cause of the
p o o r .
29 Should I not punish them for this?"
   declares the Lord.
"Should I not avenge myself
   on such a nation as this?

30 "A horrible and shocking thing
   has happened in the land:
31 The prophets prophesy lies,
   the priests rule by their own authority,
and my people love it this way.
   But what will you do in the end?

re-
h
5

Is there anyone who is prepared

To speak the truth and weep

As another black brother and sister

Lay dead, murdered in the street?

Must our children inherit this nation's wickedness?

Must another generation be blind because we are

    Too busy

    Too comfortable

    Too power hungry

Lord, rend our hearts

Were it simply a problem amongst the wicked
Perhaps then we could bear it
But it is God's people!
Those who claim his name, it is his church that
      Ignores
      Excuses
      Passes by

More blood is on our hands, our clothes stained with guilt

Lord, you continue to call your people to turn away
You have stricken us and shown us the destruction of our evil ways
Yet we refuse to be corrected, we are
      Too idealistic
      Too consumeristic
      Too individualistic
      ...dislocated and distant from one another's pain

Lord, rend our hearts

Lord rend our hearts

Like lepers - our body wastes away
And we do not even feel it
We throw parties and celebrations
Counting who has the largest crowd
          Hoarding influence
          Seeking pleasure
          Chasing admiration

Stone hard faces, we refuse to repent

And another year passes by
Black mothers, sisters, fathers, and brothers
Weep over their murdered sons and daughters
Killed while they radiated beauty, as they
          Jogged
          Rested
          Played in parks
          Walked home from school

Lord, rend our hearts

We welcome lions and wolves
In from the jungles and the deserts
We comply, we're complicit
As life continues to be devoured
      Generation
      After generation
      We forsake you
      ....so do our children

We swear by gods that are no gods

Awaken us, Oh Lord
Remove the blinders from our eyes
Take the deceit from our lips
Bring us low
      May we tremble in your presence
      Our rebellious hearts softened
      Take our riches, our power, our pride
      Have it all

That we might marvel at your costly grace

Awaken us to be a people
Who seek justice
Defend the oppressed,
And promote the cause of the fatherless
Remove the foxes we invited into your holy garden
Expose the fox inviters who love the fox more than the fruit

Lord, lead us to repentance

DISTRACTIONS OF THE MIDDLE CLASS

Lord every few months
At least once a year
Our screen is filled
With images
Our soul simply cannot bear
Black bodies, dead
Blood flowing across our screen

Enraged we cry
"I'm tired"
We lament
Please not another face
Expressing our nation's
Murderous appetite

And then the kids come home
from school
Our emails chirp,
Another meeting
Spreadsheets, groceries

Average marriages, at best
Petty conflict redirects energy
Middle class problems become front and center
As we stress over shuffling kids back and forth
Like our living room furniture
To an absurd amount of activities
And another year goes by

We find ourselves angry at the friend or family
Who ignore such gross atrocity
Our tears flow at their dismissal
But we ignore our own internal dismissal
And move on in surface tension
With short attention spans
Our heads whip quickly back
To refocus on the life and problems
Of the middle class

Apathetic, with sluggish unfit bodies
No tolerance for pain
Unwilling to endure longsuffering
And even death
So that new generations can emerge
There are just too many
Distractions
For the middle class

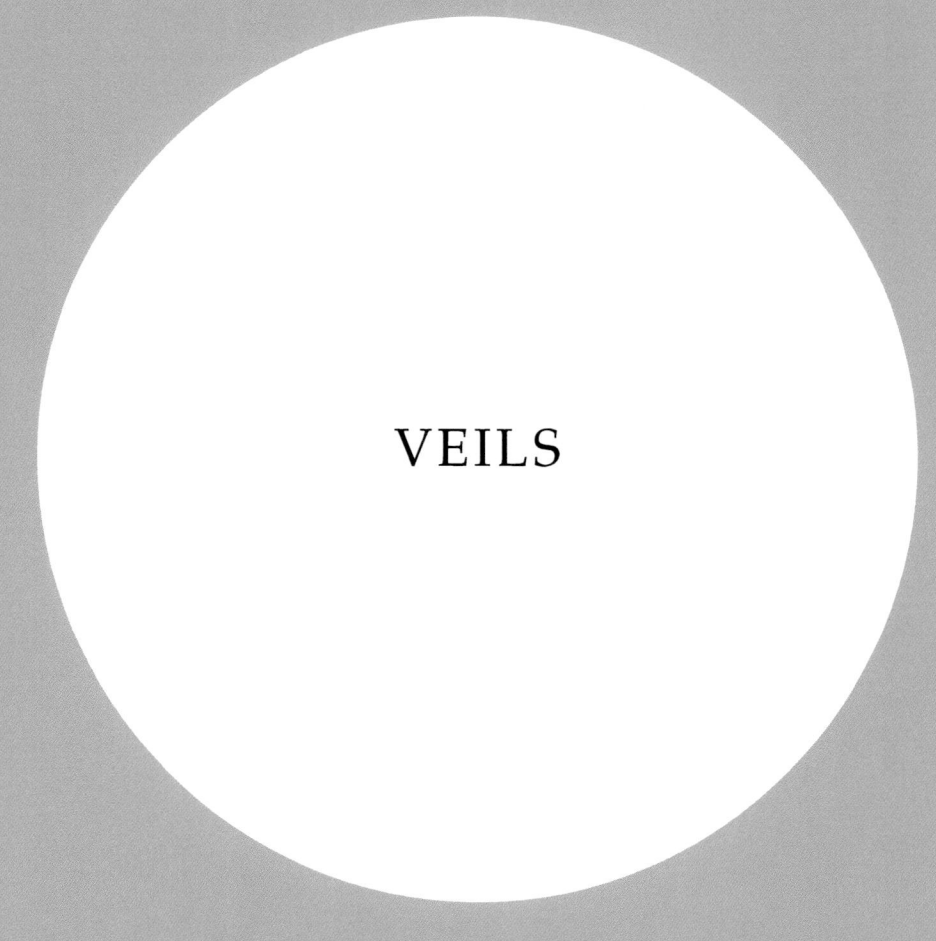

VEILS

"There is a veil"
Howard Thurman says

Of hate that separates us from one another
Black and white, rich and poor
Because we cannot see
Our imaginations run wild

As long as you are on the side
That has the power
You forget there is another life
On the other side
Of the veil
And assume all things are fine

But every now and then
There is a tear, blood seeps through
Horrified you cry
What is going on behind that veil?
Disturbed, disgusted, ashamed
But rarely is there broken surrender
Hearts cracked open, pockets emptied
Falling prostrate to the ground
Asking to do whatever can be done
To bring down
the veil

Instead the powerful stand back
And seek to mend the tear
Fearing what will happen
What might be the cost
If they tear down the veil

They come and clean the blood
Take the body away
We peek through the crack
To find the sliver of green grass
Relaxed, we're thankful
And patch up the tear
Now we don't have to see the bodies
Piling high just outside of sight
Behind the veil

TOO SMALL A WORLD

Our world is too small

Economic crisis, violence, mass death
Our minds struggle to show concern
when the stories come from outside
the walls of our own nation

We are sojourners in this place
No allegiance can be pledged
Jesus' kingdom is our only home

We analyze, debate
make plans and ideate
unaware of the ways our actions
impact the lands of our neighbors
What responsibility do we have
to the poor and suffering of the world?

That question is not simply directed to our nation
but it is a question to God's people
who reside and have been given power in this land

what responsibility
do we have to the
poor and suffering
of the world?

Our brothers and sisters flee
from violence
with sore feet
and displaced families
They migrate
leaving behind war,
loved ones,
aromas, foods
language, and lands

We too are aliens, foreigners
We should not only be fluent
in the language of our present nation
Our native language should be that of heaven
which recognizes the sounds of the world's hell
translating a welcome
to migrating and suffering souls

It is not strangers who arrive at our city gates
and border walls
but often it is
fellow citizens of heaven
or it is those, who have not yet heard
the good news of God
they come asking for our help

Our world is too small
if what we are most concerned about
lives within the boundaries
of this small nation

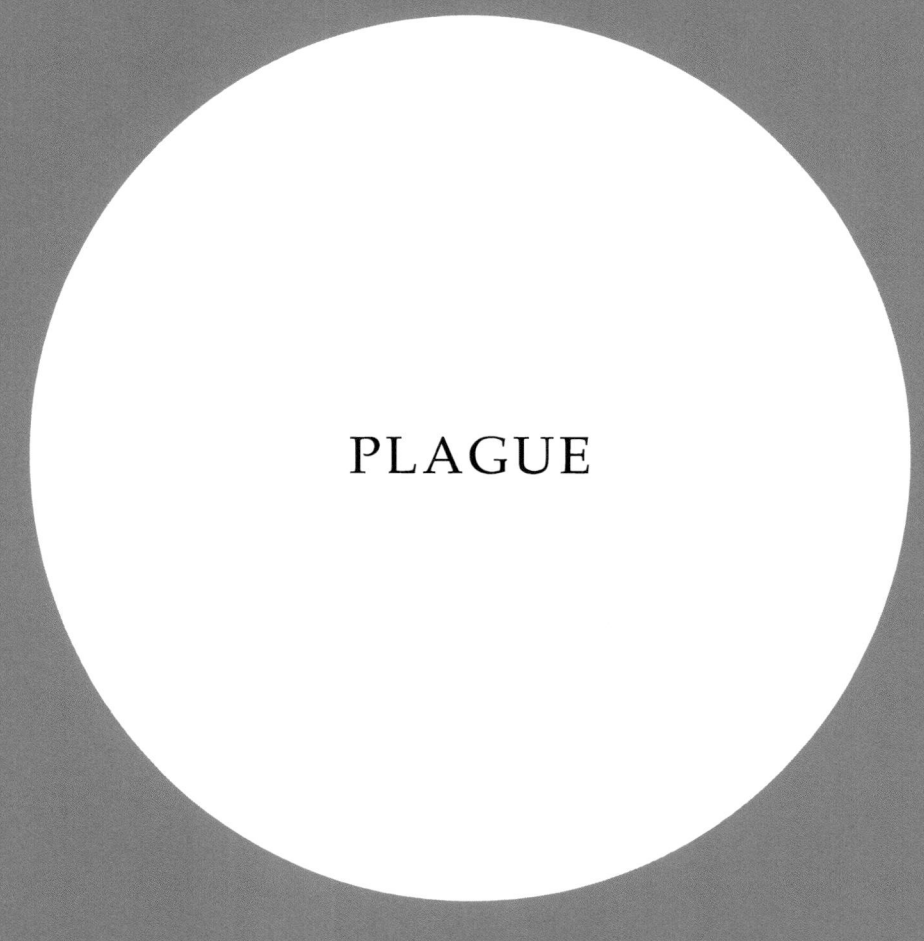

PLAGUE

Even with the fear of death
While bodies pile high
We clamor for attention and seek comfort
In objects that have no soul
Even with the aches and cries of our neighbors
Ringing in our ears,
We turn our face to power
Hoping it will save us
Seeking approval among the wealthy
Even while their harmful ways
Impacts the weakest among us
We ignore the vulnerable and "unimportant"
Making time for the powerful and privileged

Have you flattened an uneven path?

AS THE
WEALTHY
& POOR

Known and unknown
All come face to face

With death?
Together we anxiously pause
But only for a moment
Then we find ourselves too restless
Too bored, uncomfortable
To wait for deeper encounter
With you
And the poor

Humble us and lead us to repentance
Expose our deeper longings
So our hearts may be steadfast
Heal us, deliver us, have mercy on us
And until this plague relents,
Guide us in the light of your loving presence
Guide us with the light
That has always been near
The sick, destitute
And abandoned of this world

DO YOU LOVE YOUR
WHITE FAMILY?

"

do you love
their soul
enough to
ask them to...
repent

"

Will you ever ask that family member
Friend or church
To turn away from
Their supremacy
And ignorant speech

Do you love their soul enough
To ask them to repent
Of racism
And white nationalism
Or are you simply content
To gather and break bread
Thanksgiving feasts
Birthdays, weddings, funerals
Pictures snapped, you smile

Are you disturbed?
Or are you just a little more reserved
Do you share their same beliefs
And "too Christian" to be so brash?
Or still after all these years
Are you too blind and deaf
To know how their pride hurts
And oppresses the weak?

Do you love them enough to be
Filled with kindness and love
So that you can courageously say,
        "Repent
        Stop hiding, raging
        You are not the victim
        Your words expose your heart
        That has lost its love for God
        Exchanging intimacy with
        black and brown brothers
        For pharisaical religion"

As years go by,
I've made internal peace
With those who foolishly resist
the dignity and power
Within black and brown skin
I know my God will avenge
But how do I relate
To those of you who say you hear and see
But remain silent?

Lord keep me tender
I confess while feeling tired
Cracks emerge that make it easy
For bitterness to enter
Keep the soil soft
Quick to surrender
My own judgments
So that I might receive your love and grace
Believing you alone must drop the veil
Leading us to repentance,
Repair and by your grace
Reunion

GEORGE FLOYD

George Floyd

I wonder what our brother
George Floyd thought
As he sat and watched
The news unfold
Of Ahmaud's murder

Did he think the same thing
many with black skin
have wondered?
"Will I have to be the one
for the nation to see
That this is a consistent,
everyday
catastrophe?"
Did he lament to his family
Share the anger and resignation
So many of us felt
When Ahmaud was murdered?

And then the news of a sister
Breonna Taylor
Came across the screen
Daughters and mothers
Have always been a target
Of white violence
From those in power
And yet again we're here
Mourning the loss
Of another

Did our brother Floyd
Lament in silence
Asking God
"When will this end?"
Then turn off the screen
Walk to his car
And feel the shared tension
Of so many in our nation?
Having become accustomed
To the never ending violence
Knowing each year passes by
Black people die
While the world complies

Did he drive to work and pray
"Keep our sons
and daughters safe"
While brothers and sisters
Who shared his faith
Expressed concern
Not for black lives as a whole
Just this isolated "shocking" incident
of Ahmaud's murder

And did George Floyd wonder,
"When will they see,
it's not just here and there
But everywhere?
Will it take someone like me
Being murdered?"

With each event
That lights up the

SKY

We imagine the loss
Of our own sons and
daughters

Becoming widows
Losing fathers and mothers
And even if we don't expect
It to hit our very door
Generations being formed
Through violence and deliverance
Means we feel it's personal
Because it is

So while I lament
And grow weary
Wishing they'd wake up
Spirit of the Living God
Calm the raging storm in me
May I sit in your hand
Commit my spirit
To your will knowing
Not one drop of blood
Will go unavenged
And give me the strength
To faithfully resist the violence
Even if it will not be my generation
That enters the promised land

HOARDING POWER

p

o

w

e

r

Power, a gift from God

————————— Distributed in pieces to the world

Embedded in the garden

So that together, with him, we might rule and

subdue

Like a mosaic made of many stones
When brought **TOGETHER**

And exchanged
God's people bear witness
To the kingdom of Christ's love
This is how the God of the universe
Designed his power
To work in his garden

Power--important, necessary, worthy
Designed to work
Only when it's placed beneath
And quickly released to
Uplift **ALL** within the land

It's simply a utility
It has no beauty in and of itself
There is nothing about it that is too special
Average and ordinary
It has quite the common look

Power--Like a cement block
It's simple purpose is to build
So that we might cohabit
An equitable and just place
In harmony with one another
But **power by itself**
Has very little luster

Tragically, power
Like the serpent who whispered in the
garden
Comes to us and says:

       "I'm not ordinary, in fact
       You can't exist without me.
       Don't let me go.
       Consume me
       You don't have enough,
       Take some of the others
       And no matter what
       Fight til your death
       to never lose me"

Power--like a cement block
Was designed to uphold the beautiful
A gift given to lift weak things
High for all to see
To quietly serve another
Displaying and drawing attention
To what it holds,
Not itself

But instead power *whispers* like that snake:
    "Why are you holding up
    Such a weak vase?
    Go collect and *hoard more blocks*
    Take them from beneath
    Instead place them on top
    Don't lift up the fragile art
    Have everyone look at power
    Possess it, use it
    Abuse it
    Put it at the head
    Whatever you do
    Just don't lose it

The cost will not be too great
Just a few fine hair fractures
Will slowly grow down the vase
Sometimes the weight will even
Cause that vase to shatter
Collateral damage, that's ok
Hoarding power is what matters"

But as power
A gentle and precious gift
Is moved from beneath
Reaching out to hold up the sides
Instead is hoarded at the center
Placed at the top
What remains is that cement block
Lifted high
And then we bow in worship

SACRIFICING ALL

————————*EVEN* our children

Because we cannot bear to lose it

But it's not simply the ones who hoard power

Who want to possess it

But the snake slides by the weak

And reminds them of the times

They **UNJUSTLY** had their **RIGHTFUL** gifts

Possessed

They tasted at young ages

The feelings that emerged

When the little power they had

Was taken, exploited, dismissed

Or they are reminded the cost to their people

The disdain as their neighbors

Listened to their broken language

And organized to keep away

Their collective power

The serpent reminds them
the sting of shame remains
And the only way to erase it
Is to find a way to possess

P

O

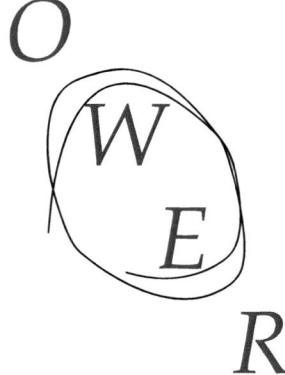 W

E

R

Distant, at the center
It feels so far out of reach
      "So climb the mountain"
      The serpent says, "and grab
      The very thing that fractured your people
      And brought your soul so much pain
      You will use it better
      When you get to the top and possess
      More power."

Father, forgive us for hoarding power

Help us to release our passionate grip

Like Christ who poured out **ALL** his power

On an oppressive cross

Might your Spirit show us

How to hold power

In sacrificial service

Distributed to every person

Unlocking the hidden potential

The power embedded within each member

Of your creation

And then we can watch in awe

As Christ reigns

And rules the kingdom

In power

LOST LOVE

what does righteousness require

As blood stains the streets, again
That could easily belong to my son or daughter
I look you in the face
And wonder
What does righteousness require?

The ignorance that flows from your mouth
The seeds of division sown
No capacity to listen
Only loud opinions
Sounding like clanging symbols
To deflect your part
Release your guilt

What tenderness was pricked
inside you? **To cause you**
to walk away

And hide behind
your "rightness"

While the one you long ago rocked to sleep
Weeps

This is an old story
Unable to repent
Of sins from past events
It is easier to become the victim
Of black people's discontent

You walk away an enemy
Your foolishness breeds hostility
What does righteousness require?
Courage to speak
Begging you
Please, do not continue to cross these lines

May God give me the capacity
To keep my head bowed low
Repenting when I nurse my wounds
Seeking him alone to bind them
So that I might still honor you
Despite the pain I've known
And the distance hostility grew between us
Because that is what righteousness requires

BLACK AND BROWN SOLIDARITY

BLACK & BROWN
SOLIDARITY

BLACK & BROWN SOLIDARITY

Brown and white
Sometimes at war within my home
One considered dirty
The other one supreme
It was not always conscious
Sometimes subtle, but not always
Jokes, dismissals, refusals to accept
Those who longed for their distant land

Perhaps I saw it in the city
Even as a kid
Because it happened inside my home
But also it's not exactly easy
To break it into something defined
One the victim, the other violent
The lines were far too blurry

Self-hatred bred participation
In this disfigured system
To push down the brown
And then we met our first black friends
Seeds of division sown
Inviting s e p a r a t i o n
Instead of solidarity
Among our suffering peoples

Superiority creates ladders
Prescriptions given to comply
Plenty of the white folks were **KIND**
BUT chose **IGNORANCE**
Never taking the time to understand

But others were hurtful and obstinate
Growing worse with time gone by
Somehow God found me in this broken place
Invited me to confess and learn to resist
Supremacy
Through black and brown
Solidarity

So even while my people suffer,
Fleeing violence
In their lands
We welcome these precious strangers
But that can never be a pass
From standing with my black sisters
And my brothers
No part will we play in this supremacy
Let me instead follow you
As we dismantle this ladder

TOGETHER

PREPARING THE BOLD TO SPEAK TRUTH TO POWER

I CONFESS

the siren's tune is loud
Forgive me for when I'm enchanted by the song of power
Too fearful to speak what you ask

Sometimes, I am afraid
What if speaking means
Prematurely surrendering power
If only I could trust my motives
And the words were simple obedience
Then I would not mind paying
Whatever the price

But I know myself
I'm stubborn, obstinate, proud
Sometimes I do not care
If it all burns to the ground
They call it passion,
But more honestly
It's often anger and unrighteous indignation
Forgive my pride
The ways I'm blind
To all that is going on inside

I do not want to squander
The gifts you've generously given
And waste power because
Childishly, I lack the self-control
To guide my tongue
Casually throwing away position
Not listening to your call
To be still

Sometimes, I am afraid
My low grade rage
Is hard to keep at bay
Yet you are always near
To expose, forgive
Transforming my tongue
Revealing my pride
Filling my self-inflicted wounds
With Christ's abiding love
To sustain and guide

How can I trust these words

Are ones you gave me

To speak….right now….this way?

Not just my opinion and impatience

TOUCH MY LIPS AND FILL ME WITH

Then confirm them through the Word made flesh

WORDS

And my fellow brethren

Because I confess, I am afraid

That the powerful will never be able to receive

From someone as weak as me

And that the deafness at times feels eroding

And my ego will react

So please I need your Spirit

To create a deeper well of peace and love

Inside me

Christ you prophetically critiqued
But also bound wounds
Ultimately dying on that cross
Delivering us from judgement
Forgive me for being judge of your beloved
Give me growing capacity
To daily lay down my life
Not just expose what is wrong,
But point to the hope
Of your healing and restoration

And so as I prepare to speak these words
Don't let me be like Jonah
Raging against the wicked thing
As though I am not also guilty
I will speak, and guide, and walk alongside
With my brothers and my sisters
Into the raging sea
Wherever your spirit guides
Please just make sure that the words I speak
Are not merely my intuition
Or anxious need to change the world

But simple obedience to your will
Words distributed for healing
That is the place I long to be
With innocence,
Serpently wisdom
Without fear of myself or them
Simply motivated by the joy that is found
In depending on you

TO GUIDE MY EVERY WORD

PREPARING THE TIMID TO
SPEAK TRUTH TO POWER

ALL I HEAR IS
CRASHING WAVES

A calling to escape
Dangers lurking in the waters
I confess I am too fearful of power
To speak with boldness when you ask

Sometimes, I am afraid
What if speaking means I will lose it all?
Security and comfort
Or even worse, affirmation?
I tremble because

I know myself

I'm timid, sometimes I lack integrity

I am too adaptive with my words

I pride myself in being nuanced

I deeply want to be seen

As the one who sees all sides

But more honestly

I also long to be competent and right

Forgive me of my striving

And the ways I'm blind to all

That is going on inside

I do not want my life to waste away
Going along the current of these unjust waters
Only reacting emotionally
When there is obvious tragedy
But lacking the courage
To learn, understand, and speak
I'm tired of ignoring the call to stand

Sometimes, I am afraid
Because in the past I've caught myself
Moving far too slowly
To win more praise by those in charge
Or just far too often
That I go along with what I know is wrong
Participating in harm

Somehow I care more about

Walking away with

A conscience appeased

Ensuring no loss of influence

GIVING LITTLE THOUGHT TO

Deep down I know, **WHAT MY LORD**

My diplomacy and silence **REQUIRES**

Is self-righteous pride

And deep insecurities

Yet in God's kindness,

He always draws near,

Reveals, forgives

Transforming my insecurity

Loosening my tongue

Growing in me a hunger

To become proficient in his righteous ways

So, God of the oppressed,
I confess, I need you to introduce me
More deeply to your heart
To trust that it is you who are powerful
Whether the spiritually deaf and blind
See, hear, or turn from their wicked ways
You are the one who is mighty to save

So if I lose everything along the way
End up exiled to the wilderness
I need to be reminded
That you go before me
I ask you to give me words to warn the powerful
Reminding them that one day
The spiritually blind and deaf will fall

Fill me with love for them
Give me the compassion to warn
And capacity to speak

GIVE THEM EARS TO HEAR

IN PANDEMIC, THE
CHURCH NEEDS MOTHERS

THE CHURCH NEEDS MOTHERS...

As we face pandemic
Death, suffering
The church needs mothers
Teaching us how to lead

Around cities
Leaders claim
This is a season of

Opportunity
Excitement
Innovation

But behind closed doors there's panic
Mothers can give definition to these words
Interpret it through
the pulsating pain
Emerging from
Neighborhoods and homes

Death, suffering, financial loss
Great cities of our world
Begin to taste
Spiritual mothers are made
To enter this space
But their words will be ordinary
Suspicious of optimistic charisma
With sacrificial beauty
They will enter
Present to the pain

A strong and compassionate mother
Can't see death and suffering
Coming to her family
And do anything but weep

Through tears, she moves toward those she loves
She scrapes together
Whatever she has
To help
Alleviate or minimize the impact
For the sake of her family
And because of her Christly encounter
She holds onto hope

Mothers are first
To comfort
Mourning
In their household
With the same tenderness
In which God comforts them
She remains resilient
With a confidence that this too shall pass
With eyes to the future she knows
Beauty always emerges from ash

She has vision
But because she is present
To the sufferings of today
She humbly knows at best
Her vision is blurred by tears

She knows it will slowly focus
As she is faithful to take
One step at a time
In obedience toward the future
That is emerging in the distance

Does disaster bring about....

Opportunity?

Yes, our spiritual mothers say
But perhaps the word would be used
With a mixture of hope and lament
There is opportunity that emerges
Whenever catastrophe strikes
When their children experience
A small or major trauma
Mothers will tell you
They watch their kids mature overnight
Becoming tender places
In which God meets, prunes and grows
Brings about something new
So in that sense, yes,
In all suffering there is opportunity
Graciously emerging
Out of things not being the way they should
We receive this gift with gratitude
All the while befriending grief

Does disaster bring about....

Excitement?

No.
That word cannot be used
To describe such a painful season
Spiritual mothers might suggest a different word
Adrenaline? Maybe.
Exhaustion? Yes.
Hope? Always.

Not excitement
Excitement is what the movies
Romantically want others to believe
Great military men feel
Right before they go to war
But spiritual mothers will tell you
That's not real

In the face of death,
These men are only boys
Pumped full of adrenaline and fear
Perhaps desire to be a hero

We need Spiritual mothers
In this pandemic
To make space for all this adrenaline
To breathe

Innovation?

Sure, mothers might use that word
It is after all a muscle
That must constantly be exercised
In the midst of devastating loss

But you'd hardly use the word
To describe this season
In ways that sound boastful
It's not quite like a business owner
Who must innovate
To make more profit

Spiritual mothers will tell you
It is more like the kind of innovation
A child growing up in the slums
Must do to scrape food together for his sister

How might a tender and strong mother
Sit down church leaders
And ask them to pause and take a breath
To prepare for the storm that is to come?
To be attentive, prepared, equipped,
Discerning for the impact this will have on those around?

The church does not need
Generals or military strategists
CEOs or entrepreneurs
Some skills like that may be helpful
You will find such competencies in mothers
Who employ military and entrepreneurial skills
In any given week as she cares for those she loves
But it's not the role she fills
And this is not a season in which the church needs
Generals, military strategists, and entrepreneurs
In suffering we need...

Mothers
Attentive, gritty, meek, discerning
Not idealists, but always hopeful
Not defeated, but pressing on
How might the Spirit meet us
In this place of disruption if we
Ensure the church listens to their
Mothers

FATHER'S DAY

Everywhere we look we see
Men and women
Boys and girls
Who are fatherless
Absent, abusive, empty, selfish
Fathers
Ignoring, abdicating
Generations
Chasing the wind
Pursuing money, pleasure
Independence
Leaving us to raise ourselves
Fatherless

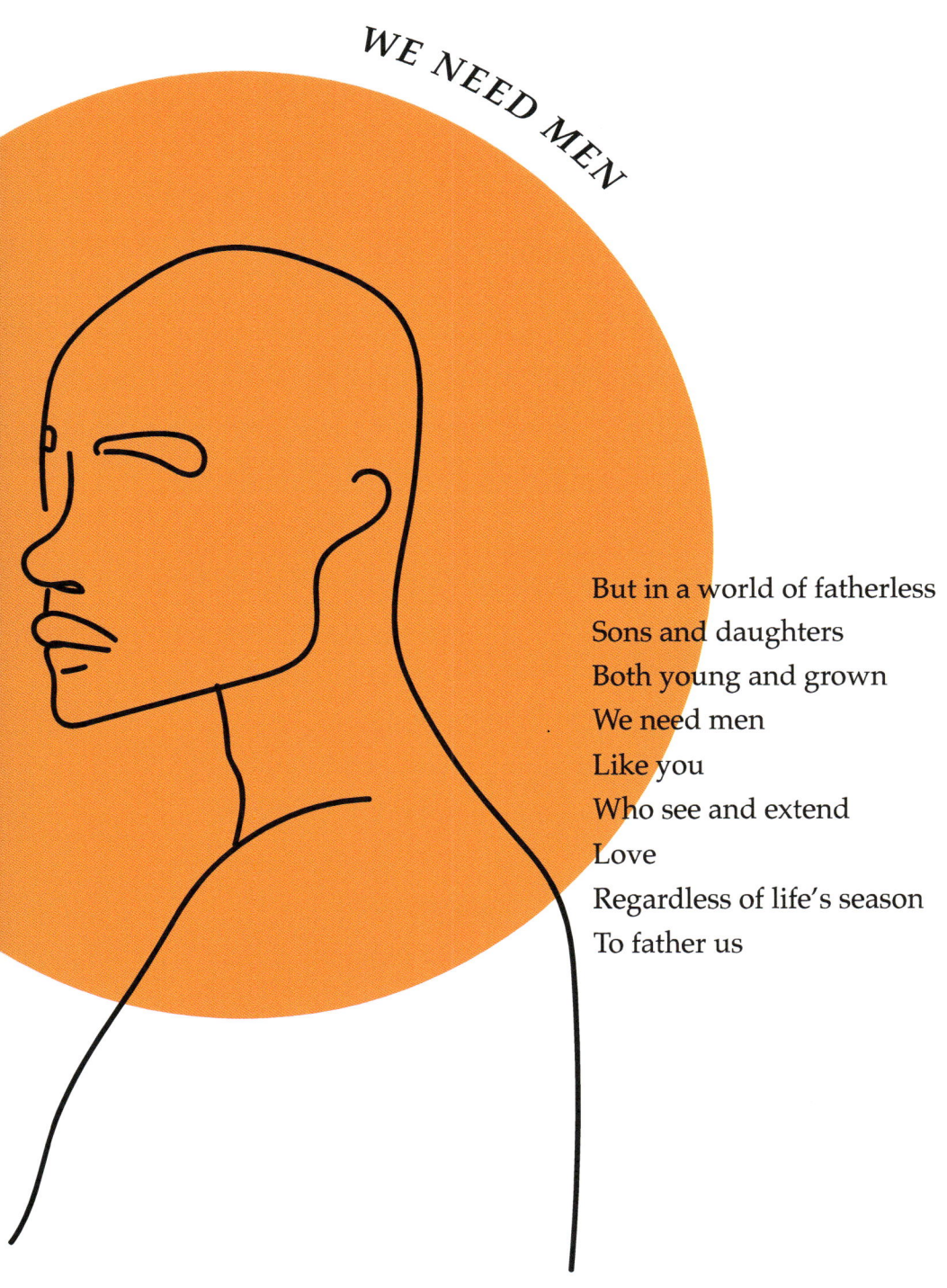

WE NEED MEN

But in a world of fatherless
Sons and daughters
Both young and grown
We need men
Like you
Who see and extend
Love
Regardless of life's season
To father us

Carrying burdens to provide
Learning to trust
Their Great Provider
Increasing generosity
Expanding their protection
To include the ones
Who go unprotected
Leading with conviction, compassion
Directing with vision
Strong enough to stand
And fight
Fire
Filled with hope
Pursuing community
That includes more
Then their own flesh and blood
So that generations
Of the fatherless
Can see

HEALING HOLY LOVE

Our Father in heaven—
Sacrificial, generous
Present, near
Strong
Full of healing holy love
Slow to anger
Abounding joy
Through his Son
Brings the fatherless
Into himself
So that generations
Will know their
Father

CONFESSING CONTRADICTIONS

Forgive me Lord for each day
In which I've constructed my life
To not be in communion
Proximate
In community with the poor
Distant
From those who suffer
Show us your ways oh Lord
Lead us in the light of your everlasting love

Forgive me Lord for my self righteousness
The ways I've sold what I have
And given to the poor
Only to pride myself
As though my love somehow gets a pass
Because my deeds look so righteous
What kind of gospel is that?

"WITHOUT LOVE IT JUST BECAME ~~RELIGION~~"

Forgive me Lord for the ways I've spoken
Wisdom, uttered prophecy so glorious
Sacrificing my body to hardship
But without love it just became religion
Create in me a clean heart
Renew a righteous spirit within

Might my longings for your righteousness remain
Receiving the gifts you've embedded within the poor
Speaking up for the voiceless
But from a humble and quiet place
Enjoying the blessings of your good creation

FORGIVE US FOR
BEING A DISAPPOINTING
COMMUNITY

You entered community
With high hopes
Longing to find friendship
And family
But instead, you discovered insecurity
And petty spirituality

A shared identity
Around niche interests
No space for real communion
Perhaps leaders demanded
Your admiration
And when you fell short
Or seemed not to be a fit
You were no longer welcome

you left a little wounded

Disillusioned, discontent
What is the purpose of gathering
When what we see
Is just merely the surface
Of discontented spirituality

The offering plates were passed around
No matter how much you suffered
They promised you a reward

"Give, bless the Lord's work,
We promise you'll receive ten fold in return"

Give honor to the leader
Praise his divine connection
Don't doubt him
His job is just so hard
Make sure you stroke tender
Fragile, frail, and fractured egos

Perhaps you received some gifts
It was not all so bad
But still when you arrived
It felt not quite like what you had in mind

We can be a disappointing community
Brother who has wandered off
Sister who is unsure about returning
Forgive us

It should not be a surprise
That our spiritual lives
Would include something
As ordinary
Fragile and frustrating
As being in something as simple and average
As community
What makes you ache
And expect more
Is deep inside you know
Communal space is where
The mystery of transformation occurs

Forgive us for misusing
Leadership
Making it about our own stories
Instead of *all* God's people
It is not only professionals, pastors
Theologians or musicians
But it's all who hold God's gifts
Distributed to every single one
And until the people are awakened
To the collective calling of the saints
Until the shepherds and the prophets
Truly speak God's word
No longer seeking selfish gain
Then we will continue to be
Disappointing community

And where there is not yet place to risk
And expose our need for the other
We will mourn our anemic faith
Unable to receive the gift of doing life
Deeply embedded within community

Forgive us for being a disappointing community

Your longing for more is good
Somehow through
Ordinary, simple
Moments of confession
May Christ knit us together
To be a new and vibrant
Family

A CONFESSION FOR
BROTHERS AND SISTERS

all:

Forgive us
For not being true brothers and sisters
For letting the pollution of this world
Create smoke and mirrors
Distorting our holy body
Into an object to devour
A thing to look at
And consume
Forgive us for not being
Brothers and sisters

Forgive us for thinking your image
Is simply a masculine expression of power
And forgetting the tenderness in which you gather us
Like hens beneath your wing
Forgive us for not being
Brothers and sisters

sisters:

Forgive us, the Sisters
For softening our voice
So we don't disrupt the powers
For diminishing our worth
For struggling and striving
Fighting misuse of power
With words that aren't healing
Forgive us for settling
For exposure of injustice
Without desiring restoration
Or instead adopting ignorance
Thinking that might be safer

Forgive us, the Sisters,
For seeing other sisters as a threat
For the times we are the first to enter space
And protect it as our own
Not looking for others
More gifted, strong, equipped
Or young, raw, and undeveloped
And using our power, no matter how scarce
To elevate, prop up, and promote
Our sisters

Forgive us, the Sisters,
For needing another's gaze
Admiration and acclimation
As a cheap exchange
When we have the gaze of our King
Forgive us for questioning-
What good is it to be this gender?
For believing we are a hindrance,
A snare to mission

Help us, Lord,
To labor, enduring pain
Working with you to see new birth
And restoration
In our communion
Becoming
True sisters

brothers:

Forgive us, the Brothers,
For our pride and stubborn hearts
For our misuse of power
Diminishing and casting aside
Our sisters

Forgive us, Lord, for our violence
That comes from our bodies, words, and stories
For the ignorant culture we created
And sustained
Of competition and unrighteous glory
To expand our territory
Sow our spiritual oats
For only making space for those
Who stroke our frightened egos
For being afraid of insignificance
And the tender places our stronger sisters expose

Forgive us, the Brothers,
For only seeking to relate to women
As a wife, daughter or mother
Forgetting that sisters can see us
And playfully remind us of our ordinariness
In ways a romantic partner
or mother never can

Forgive us for not being first
To place ourselves beneath
Using power to showcase our sisters' strength
For abdicating our call to death
So that new life can emerge
Ignoring our sisters who writhe in pain
As they bear the weight
Of our collective sin
In their bodies, sleep, and memories

Help us, Lord,
Bring to our memories
The words, thoughts, and jokes
That diminish our sisters
So we might confess and know your grace
And the gift you embedded
Within the deep love of our sisters
Restore us
As true brothers

all:

Lord, renew our minds
Heal our bodies
Make us know the joy that is found
Within the bond of brothers and sisters
Co-laborers, co-heirs with Christ
Our dear older brother
With him reigning eternally
In union with each other

WHEN PASTORS
ABUSE THEIR POWER

Much of my Christian faith
Has been nourished and shaped,
Through the testimony and experience of others

They aren't my foundation
Christ alone is my anchor
But their words, reflections and actions
All echo from the past
They bear witness to an ancient faith
Global and near

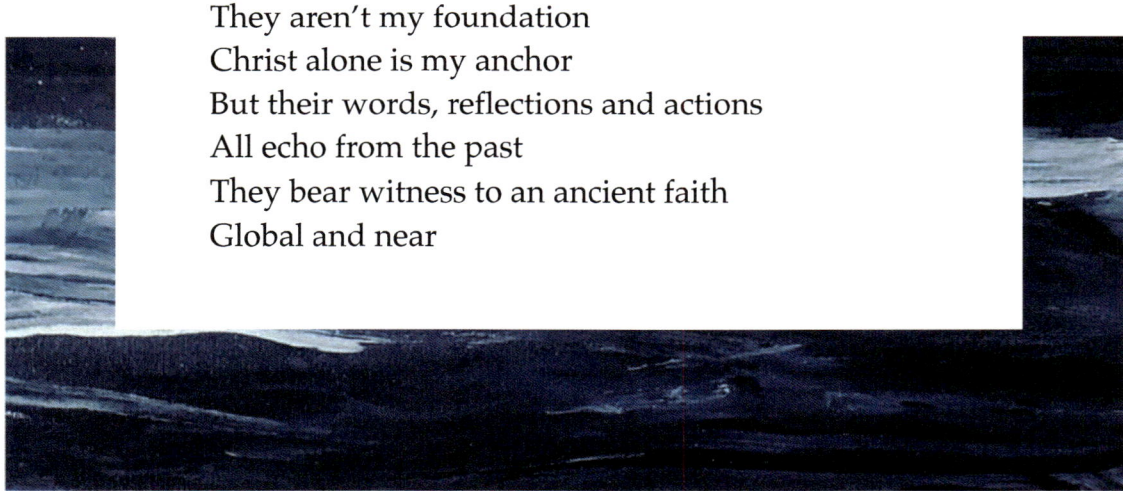

Reminding me that

EVERY SAINT
IS A HUMBLE
SINNER

And within each sinner, a hidden  saint

I'm surrounded by many loved ones
Who've left the Christian faith
Often holding tight shared values
They practice love of neighbor, self-sacrifice
Yet no longer accept the words
They once believed necessary
To sustain their life

But my life is also full of some
Who claim the name of Christ
Yet anger, fear, and judgment
Somehow distorted the Christian way
People reduced to projects,
A life of sacrifice exchanged
For propping up a platform,
Political agendas and national worship
Pursued no matter the cost
Resulting in those who don't follow Christ
Profane the name of God

As years go by mentors, friends,
Former pastors
Continue to have their life exposed
What's discovered is of deep concern,
At times much worse
These men of words and wisdom
Spoke of encounters with God that sunk deep into my heart
Experiences were shared in such a way
They became owned by those who followed

Some days it becomes hard to trust
That these powerful and holy words
Were not just made up to pursue selfish gain
Perhaps the need for admiration
Perpetuated what was only smoke and mirror
Could the explanation be so simple?
Lies retold until they sounded true
Maybe false encounters with God projected
To make their captive audience subdued
Or could it also be these true encounters somehow
Were never muted by the violence of their deeds?
Some days it's hard to see through the haze
Created by lifetimes of deception

And yet, there is the woman who bled 12 years
Then fiercely pushed her way through that crowd
The lonely Samaritan who was greeted by a thirsty rabbi
Then sent to tell the suspicious village
Of the one who had come to save
The prostitute, face bent low in shame
Who courageously snuck into the party
Washed his feet with tears
The street child straining to catch a glimpse
Who caught his eye and saw delight
As Jesus scooped him on his lap

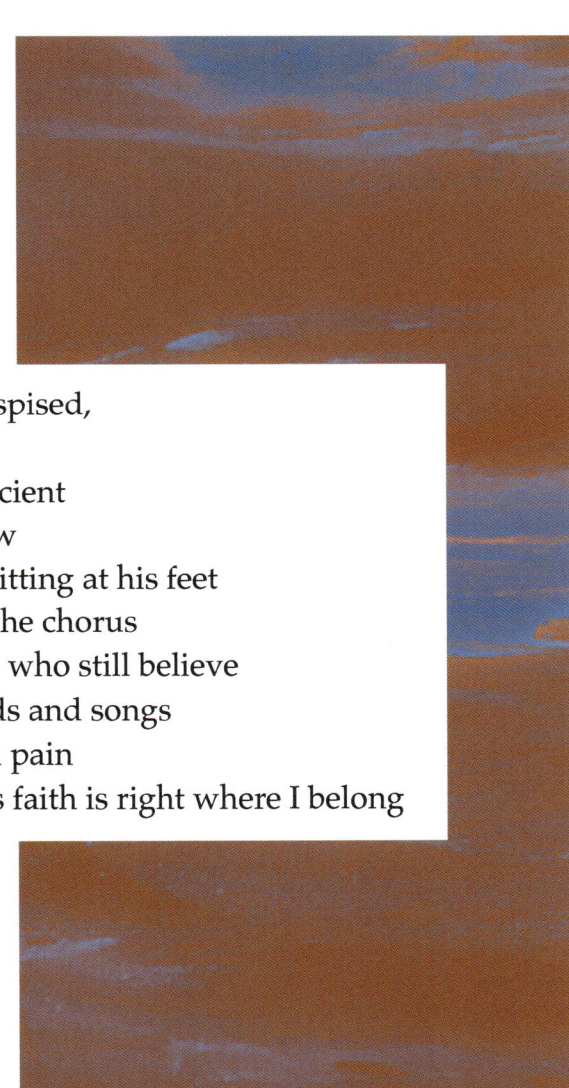

The scorned and despised,
First seen by Christ
The proud and sufficient
Invited to also follow
Join the humble in sitting at his feet
Their witness joins the chorus
Of countless friends who still believe
Friends whose words and songs
Through shame and pain
Remind me that this faith is right where I belong

And then there is the quiet voice
Whispering to me
Inviting me to look
At my open wounds and tired scars
To be honest about desires, pain,
Hopes, and longings
And release control of the image
I'm tempted to project
With honesty remember the dark shadows
That lurk beneath my surface
Remembering my savior,
With love filled eyes
Gazing deep within

Surrounded by these contradictions,
There is my true North Star-
Jesus, my closest friend
Whose words have grasped me
Kept me near
Delivered me from
Sorrow and rejection
Called me out of darkness
Wrapped me in the warmth of his loving light
And there it is with him, only him,
That my heart is at rest and safe within

HEALING JOURNEYS

pt.3

TENDER STRENGTH

the candle lit within

Violence can never overtake beauty
Though it rages like a forest fire
And burns like the sun
No matter what it scorches
Beauty will break through
And overcome

You were formed in a fire
Protected by divine love
Led out of the furnace
Into the shadow of love's wing

Singed clothes, burned skin
Restored
Strengthened
Some tender spots remain
Guided back to the furnace
Empowered now to resist
And manifest a different way

Never alone
The fiercest flame
Cannot snuff out
The gentle beauty contained
In the candle lit within

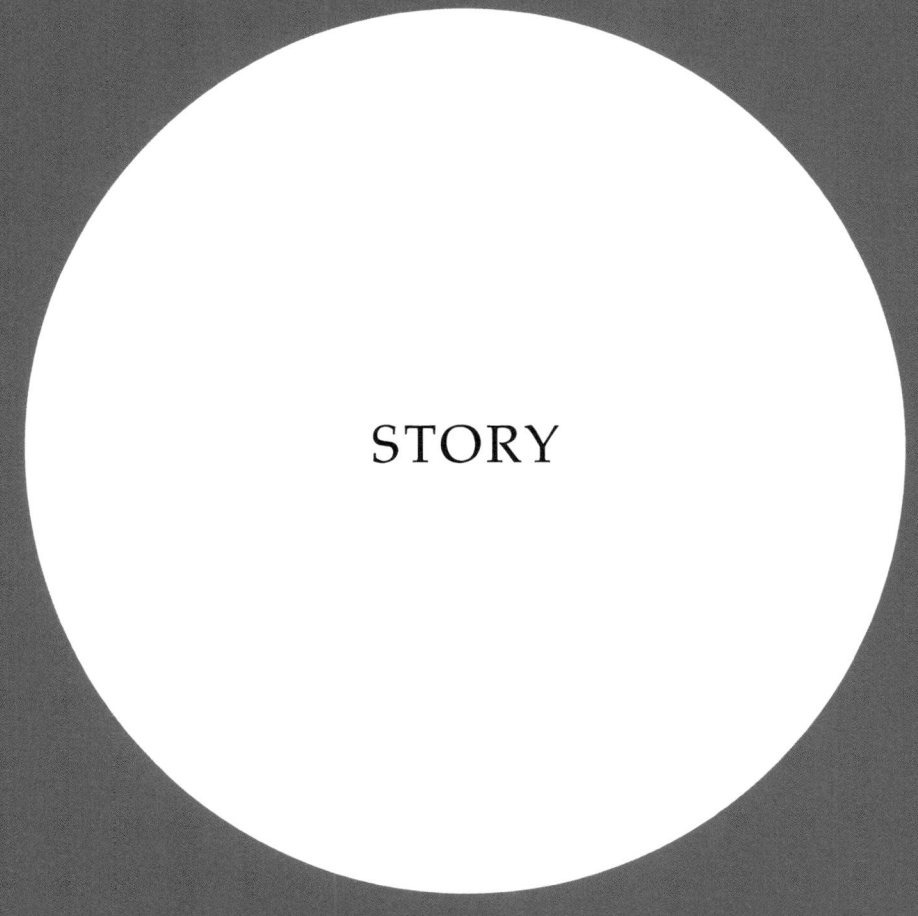

STORY

Violent hands...
Inflicting bruises and breaking bones
Or worse...
Tender, but unwelcome caresses
Shattering innocence

Destructive words....
Terrifying hearts and evoking self-contempt
Or worse...
Inviting, but manipulative
Confusing and eroding self worth

Extinguished hope....
Drown out as she struggled to keep above water
Or worse...
Unable to resist the darkness
She gave in to death

Crowded tables...
No place for her to belong, excluded
Or worse...
Perhaps it's what she deserved
She must escape

Invited...
From the bottom of the waters to breathe again
And then...
Taken by the hand and called "beloved"
Welcomed to a feast

Terrified...

She looks around and sees light break in

And then...
Light exposes wounds, scars, and stains
In the presence of Pure Love, hope is born

Affirmed...
She discovers healing words
And then…
Courage grows alongside compassion
Her head held high prepared to enter

Touched...
First by the mysterious and tender hand of God
And then….
As if that were not quite healing enough
Divine love reached through children, friends,
And, most of all, her life companion
Restored her innocence

LONELINESS

Loneliness,

she is your friend
Do not fear her
Though the ache is crushing
And the temptation to dismiss her grand

She is longing
Hidden within you
She is desire
That cannot be fully satisfied

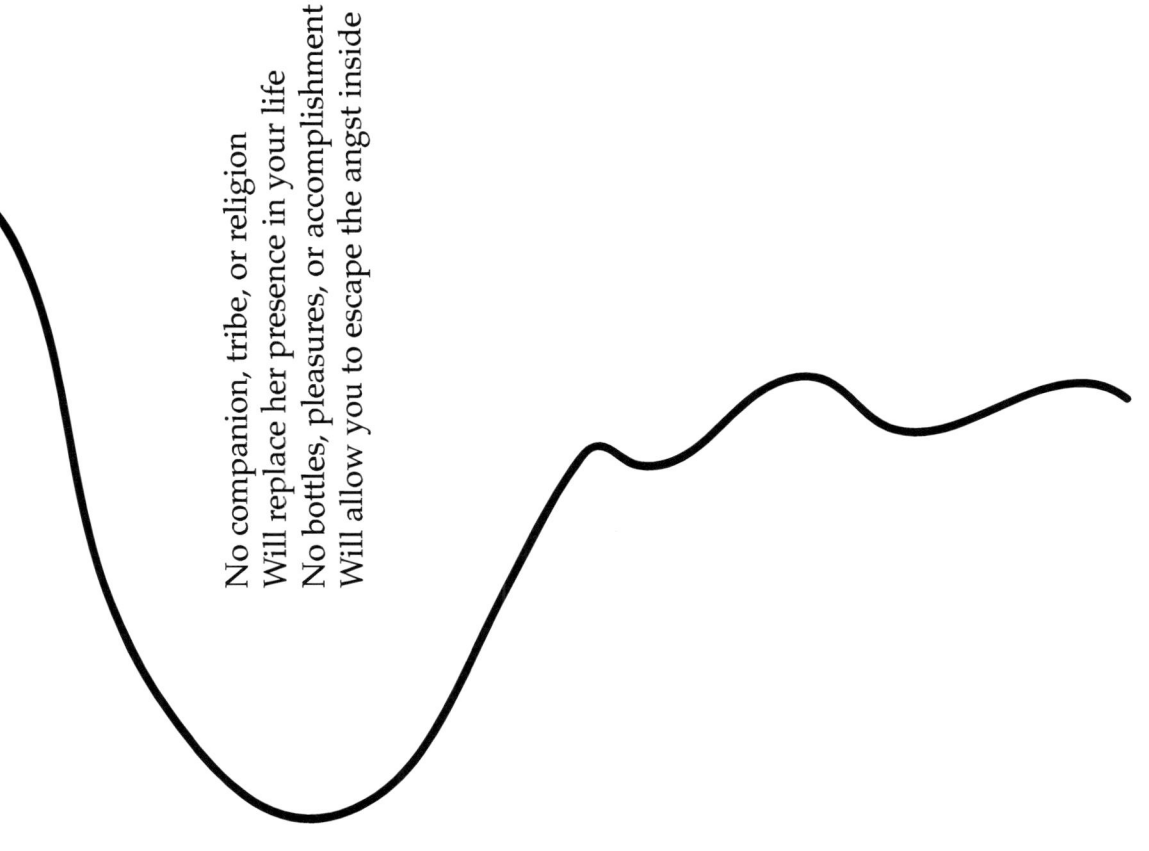

No companion, tribe, or religion
Will replace her presence in your life
No bottles, pleasures, or accomplishment
Will allow you to escape the angst inside

Loneliness, she is your friend
Become familiar with her
Do not tuck her away
Release your need to have her satisfied

It is then you will discover
She is the whisper of your Creator
Deep within your soul,
Through her voice, he calls you

Awakening you to see the greater beauty
Even in suffering
Giving you sight of hope
Even where evil casts dark shadows

It is there, that loneliness guides you
To no longer hold life with a fierce grip
Nor attempt to escape the here and now
In search of other worlds

As you open yourself to receive her gifts
You will find deeper satisfaction
As loved ones are no longer needed to make her go away
Communion no longer a mere transaction

INTRODUCTIONS

IS NEAR.

IS NEAR.

IS NEAR.

IS NEAR.

IS NEAR.

IS NEAR.

IS NEAR.

IS NEAR.

IS NEAR.

When I was little
I wandered to the playground
Scared and alone
I sat on a swing
Ashamed

Jesus sat next to me
and smiled

VICTIMHOOD

Victim

Can you step into that space?
Just for a bit
I know you're scared
It can be such a confining word
Or perhaps one that will restrict
Already the weakest in the room
The word affirms your deepest fears

But linger here, just a bit
And

DIS-COVER GOD,

THE VICT IM

Exposed
Naked on a cross
Blood flowing
Skin tearing
Humiliated, his body hangs
Abandoned on that oppressive cross

Victim

Can you enter that space knowing Jesus waits?
His own scars and open wounds look a lot like yours
Take courage
No longer hide your deepest pain
Trust his tender strength
Allow yourself compassion
And settle into his embrace

Restored

He casts aside all labels
No longer are you a victim
Just a beloved son or daughter
Tender wounds still showing
Healing scars now radiate Christ's love

VICTIM Can you loosen your grip and the need to remain here?

Victim

Can you now let go?
The word temporarily gave protection
From tragic and unjust blows
But it cannot describe all that you are
It splits the world and you in two
Unable to see your own darkness
And demanding others see your light

Victim

This word whispers a subtle lie
That exposure and humiliation of the offender
Is all that can erase those shameful wounds
But when justice is served
Or becomes impossible
If all that remains is a wounded victim
How much greater the loss

Transformed

He invites your wounds to be placed in his
He lifts your face
No longer bent low
You radiate
A crown now placed upon your royal head

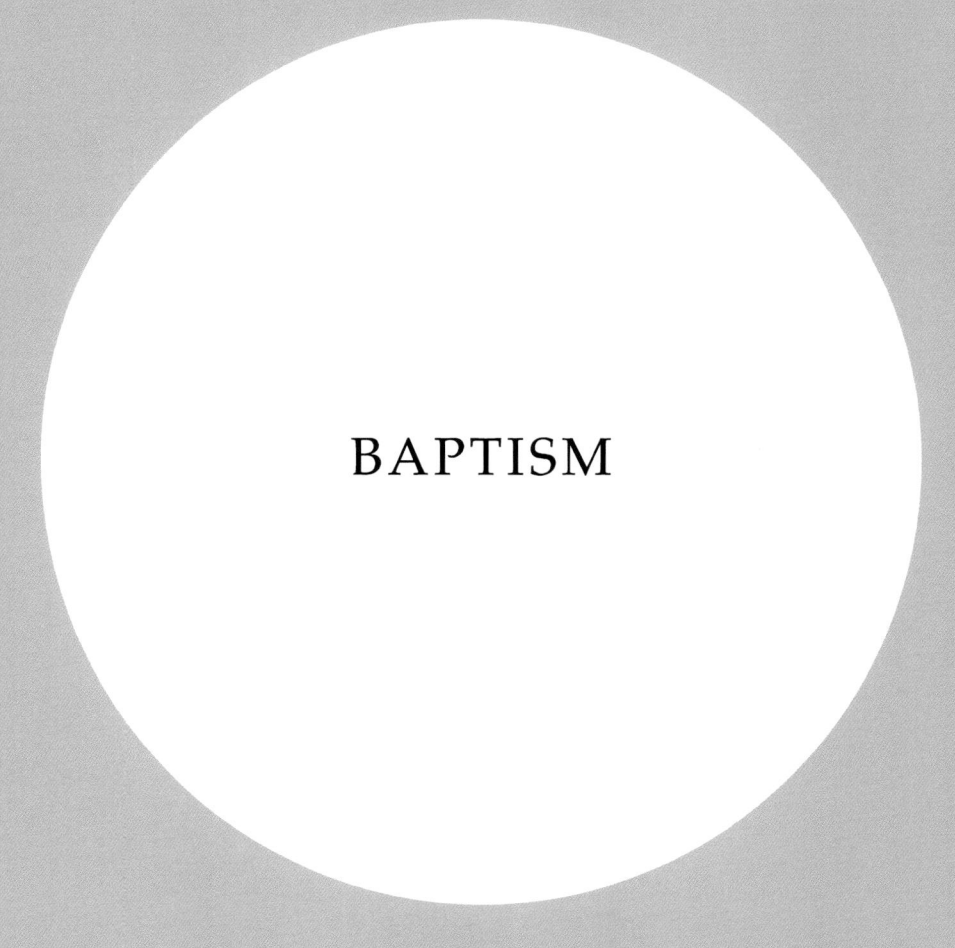

BAPTISM

immersion in water symbolizing purification

BAP-TISM

It was ten, maybe twenty seconds
You were held under the water
Struggling, pulling, pushing
Trying anything to release that grip
Darkness overwhelmed you
Clouding out the light
You were confident that this
Would be your final night

What could possess your mother
To see your existence as a threat
Why is it that your presence
Was such an awful sight?
Deep within the waters
You couldn't move or breathe

let your nakedness be exposed

And then a light
Broke into the room
Releasing the tight grip
That held you
Suffocating
Under the water

Miraculously, you can't explain it
You were led out of the waters
Into the safety of your room
Still gasping for air
Grabbing for a towel
Settling your body bruised
Into a wooden chair
Promising to never again
Let your nakedness be exposed

But then the light came back
Finding you in your room
God's holy touch
Awakened you and grew you up
Even while an enemy
Persisted in your home
No matter what kind of darkness came
Light always seemed to guide you

But there came a point where you wanted more
Covers to protect and hide you
And God kindly let you
Stay there for awhile
Projected strength, anger, achievement
Pleasure, position, and man's praise
All these covers seemed to keep you safe
Keeping fear, loneliness, and sorrow
Hidden and out of sight

But eventually you were ready
For deliverance from the lies
That your existence and presence
Is what created such resistance

Surrendering to God's hand
He guides you
Together you lower the covers
Emerging from beneath
Letting others see
The tenderness, the gentle person
Who's learning to be present
Even in front of enemies
Because darkness just can't resist
The light God placed inside

PRODIGAL FATHERS

Your prodigal child
That you abandoned
Was adopted
By a kind and loving King
At first it took a while
For her to understand
That she was no longer
An unwanted daughter

So used to defending
And striving
Pushing her way in
Fighting
Against the obscene

That when she was invited
To join this family feast

She   didn't
k   n   o   w
if   she   was
s   a   f   e

To enter in
And release all her grief

She had become accustomed
To tattered clothes
And dirty feet
Those who walked by
Seemed to see the stain
Of what she felt inside

But then a gentle King
Came looking outside the gate
For a daughter
He found her
Brought her in
And lavished love
Endlessly
Always standing beside her

She moved into the palace
At first still in dirty clothes
Despite her brand new status
Overwhelmed
It all simply felt too lavish

Some days she'd go for walks
In the royal gardens
And peek down the palace streets
She'd wait to see
If she could catch a glimpse of you
And what she might say
If you ever walked her way

She'd imagine herself with a shaken fist
Anger, disappointment, sorrow

Confronting your l——ong absence

And past actions
Feeling old memories of shame
And betrayal
But each and every time
Her new Father
Would walk up
And gently stand beside her
He'd place his arm around her
And let her have a spacious place
To yell with that stiff face

Until eventually she'd melt
Into his patient side
Reminded of his love
Through anger, disappointment
Even unforgiveness
He never left her side
"Forever you are loved"
the consistent message he gave

Slowly over time the rags were thrown away
The clothes that once felt lavish
She began to enjoy each day
And now sometimes
She wanders that same path
And peeks in the direction
Of where she knows you're at
Her imagination trails off
Wondering
If you'll ever journey to this place
And when you do
She will be ready
To welcome you

DISCOVERY

Your first encounter
Was a whisper
Mysterious
I called you
And you came

Welcomed as my child
Into my very being
Not withholding anything
But only giving you
What you were ready to receive

Tenderly I held you
Rocked you
Pressed you tightly
Against my chest
Slowly you grew older
So I took you by the hand
And led you into the forest

Still inside me
We are one
You went into the shadows
Like any good father
I'm right here
Beside you
Letting you drift off
To explore the meadows
And discover the adventure
I want to take you on
Inside you

And then
From the shadows of the forest
You hear a sneering laugh
You look back startled
What's that?
I'm here, I nudge you
Toward the shadows
But only because I know it's time
And you are willing
To enter
And uncover
The things that have been hiding

Your heart beats fast
Your body freezes
Is it really time?
To face the beasts
That have been lurking
So long within the shadows?

I wait. With you.
Calm. Patient.
I've got nothing else to do
We can wait here for eternity
But I'm also happy to go with you
Into the shadows

Terrified
You take a breath
Certain this must be the place
That you will die
But still, you go
I'm so very
Proud of you

And we walk into the forest
As the trees thicken and the light darkens
You squint and squeeze my hand
And then, like I had planned
You released it
Stumbling, you couldn't see
The darkness of the forest
Frightened you

You are stuck
Endlessly
Frozen, you can't move
How long have you been in darkness?
A month? A year? Ten?
You weep and shout
Why have you been abandoned?

Eventually your eyes adjust
To the darkness
You see me tenderly waiting
Always present
I've been here all along
Because you are inside of me
And I you
After all, we are one

You collapse in me
Again I rock you
Tenderly holding you against my chest
My dear child
You are ready
To discover the new things
I want to show you
In the shadows

Your face transforms
No longer fearful
Instead I see solid determination
And I laugh with joy
Look at you
You grew six inches taller
Your head is now held high,
Shoulders back you stand
Suddenly ready
To run into the shadows

We will be here a bit
So I can tell you the story
That is true
About these shadows
And then we will begin
The journey back
To the bright meadows

It is here you will emerge
Stronger and yet somehow more tender
Older yet more like a child
Your eyes will now struggle
Adjusting to the light
Always stinging just a little
With deeper longing for the others
To enter into their shadows
But as for you and I
We will continue to walk together
Discovering all that is inside you